Get Your Free Transformation Quadrant Workbook!

www.christinekloser.com/tq

This fill-in-the-blank workbook makes it easy to get the most out of this powerful tool. It also helps you keep track of all the insights you're about to receive for your book. Grab it now... it's free.

"The 'Transformation Quadrant' is just phenomenal! In less than an hour I got total clarity about the transformation I want for myself, my readers, my business and the world. This tool made it easy, natural and FUN to lay this foundation for my book. Plus, it gave me a boost of confidence to restart and stick to writing my book (it sat on the back burner for years). Since doing the Quadrant, I am working on my book every day!"

—**Dr. Anja Walter-Ris**
Life, Business and Success Coaching with Soul

"Like many aspiring authors convinced they have something worth sharing with the world, I was lost when it came to understanding how to make it happen. After completing my Transformation Quadrant, I was able to gain clarity on the purpose of my book, replace self-doubt with confidence and develop a practical plan to finish my book and get it published."

—**Mitch Goddard**
Founder, Goddard Life & Career
Coaching Institute

"I was fortunate to do a Transformation Quadrant consultation with Christine. When we worked on the 'reader quadrant' I was empowered to enlarge my vision, and see thousands of my readers feeling supported and encouraged at a time when they really needed it. This clarity made me understand how important it is to get my book done. I started writing it immediately after my consultation... thanks to Christine and her Transformation Quadrant."

—Hannah Anderson
Founder of Golden Thread Coaching and Consultation

"The Transformation Quadrant gave me a clear picture of how to proceed with my book about public speaking. This tool really works, and I highly recommend you use it for your book."

—James Boswell, DTM
Communication Coach

"The Transformation Quadrant helped me clarify my ideal reader and the approach to use in writing my book. As a result of creating my Quadrant, I increased my clarity about the direction, essence and depth of my book. Now, it's easy to write! I highly recommend you use the Transformation Quadrant too."

—Linda Robinson
Writer, spiritual teacher, speaker

The Transformation Quadrant®: A Ground-Breaking Author
How to 'Blueprint" Your Book in 15 Minutes of Less

 Capucia

Published by:
Capucia LLC
211 Pauline Drive #513, York PA 17402
www.capuciapublishing.com

ISBN: 978-1-945252-62-4
Library of Congress Control Number: 2019941093

Cover Design: Joseph Blalock
Interior Design: Ranilo Cabo
Editor: Gwen Hoffnagle
Author Photo: Ken Rochon, The Umbrella Syndicate

THE
TRANSFORMATION
QUADRANT

HOW TO BLUEPRINT YOUR BOOK
IN 15 MINUTES OR LESS

CHRISTINE KLOSER

Capucia LLC
York, PA

To the leaders, business owners, visionaries, coaches, healers, practitioners and messengers around the world who want to write their book and make a difference in the lives of others.

TABLE OF CONTENTS

CHAPTER 1

Laying the Foundation for Success

Hello and welcome! I'm so grateful you're reading this book, because on these pages I share my groundbreaking and transformational method to "blueprint" your book in fifteen minutes... or less.

You might be asking, "What does that mean exactly? Isn't a blueprint the same as an outline?" And I can tell you right now... it's not. It goes *much* deeper.

This blueprint – the Transformation Quadrant –is *extremely* powerful, and in fact my clients have used this exact tool to...

- Build successful businesses, some of which have hit multiple six and near seven figures
- Appear on TV and radio like ABC, CBS, CNBC, NPR, *The New York Times* and TEDx
- Sign book deals with major publishers
- Become best-selling authors in their categories
- Be invited to speak in places as far and wide as Hong Kong, Spain and Australia

But most important of all they're now recognized as thriving transformational leaders in their areas of expertise. Clients seek them out. They get emails and letters from readers whose lives they've changed.

And it all begins with creating this blueprint using a very simple fifteen-minute exercise that I'll teach you in this book. And here's the amazing thing: The Transformation Quadrant works even if you haven't written a single word of your book yet. It works even if you never *intended* to be an author, yet you recognize the power of writing a book to reach more people with your message.

Authorship gives you more credibility and new opportunities for visibility. Plus, your book can become the "key" that turns over the engine of your business.

One of my clients is an artist and had no interest in writing a book. However, she heard me speak at an event and was inspired to write! Now, because of her written and published book, she's fulfilling her dream as a workshop and retreat facilitator who combines her gift for art with her transformational message! That's the power of this blueprint.

It even works if you think you can't write. In fact I have a client whose native language isn't English, but using this blueprint she found her voice, signed a sweet deal with her dream publisher and has now built a purpose-driven book-based business where she teaches courses, hosts live events, runs a podcast and enjoys a successful private practice. And that's not all this tool can do.

As authors – first-timers or otherwise – we run into major obstacles like writer's block, self-doubt and overwhelm. We don't know how – or where – to start. We don't know if what we have to say really matters. And we have hundreds of "experts" telling us how to write our books.

It can be stressful! Writing a book is *challenging*. And it's important you know this up front because book experts will tell you that you can write a book in a weekend, go from "nothing" to best-seller in ninety days or get overnight credibility and have droves of people tripping over themselves to hire you.

Well, that's simply unrealistic. When you follow that "microwave method" of writing you can end up with a formulaic book that doesn't fully represent your best work or showcase who you truly are. Because you're reading this I know that's not what you want. And I'll tell you straight up that I can't promise you'll write a book in two days, or even in a month's time. Nor do I want you to feel like you *should* be doing that. Some of my clients have written their books in ninety days while some take three years. One of my recent clients, Sue, a corporate consultant, finished her first draft in thirty-three days. Every author is different.

But here's what I *can* promise you. With this blueprint you'll be empowered to overcome any writer's block, self-doubt or overwhelm you face. And your excuses about writing will begin to fall away – excuses like not having time, self-doubt and being confused about where to start. With this blueprint you'll know exactly what you need to do *first*, and what to do *next* – every step of the way – to make your book successful.

The amazing thing about this is that it's *not* your outline. Think of it as the "seed" of your book. And with this seed you'll create your book's outline, the structure, the chapters, your teaching system, your title, your cover and even your best marketing strategies.

That's why I say that this blueprint builds the solid foundation *beneath* your outline. Let me put it another way: If you think of your book's outline as the skeleton or structure of your book, what I'm about to show you is how to discover the *soul* – or the DNA – of your book.

And if I may be so bold, I'm going to tell you it's nearly impossible to write your best book if you don't follow this blueprint. I also want to tell you that by the end of *The Transformation Quadrant* you will have also discovered how to get the exact support you need to write that best book.

A lot of authors struggle to write. They have pages and pages of notes and research on their computer. And they certainly have dreams of writing a book. But too often they spend thousands of dollars on how-to courses, coaches and books on writing, and years or decades later they still haven't written *their* book.

I think the main reason they struggle is because they don't follow this blueprint. They don't know what the soul or DNA of their book is. My intention is for you to see exactly why having this blueprint is the *most* important thing for your book, and to provide you with next steps to take to ensure you get your blueprint done correctly from the beginning... even before you write a single word!

This isn't just about your book. You should do this for yourself as an author, for your readers, for your business and even for how your book will impact the world. What I'm about to teach you is one of my more advanced author trainings, and it isn't for everyone. The kind of books I help authors write are often in the genres of self-help, business, personal growth, relationships, leadership, spirituality and transformational fiction. If you're writing traditional fiction like romance, mystery, or adventure this tool likely won't help you. And if you're writing academic nonfiction like history, economics or politics, this isn't the blueprint to use.

But if you want to transform your readers' lives and help them grow, heal, succeed or fix their problems; if you want to make an impact in the world by sharing your wisdom and expertise; or if you're an entrepreneur, coach, practitioner or consultant who wants to take your business to the next level, what I'm about to teach you will transform the way you write your book, attract readers and clients and start or grow your book-based business.

In fact, here's a partial list of the types of authors I've helped using this kind of approach since 2004:

- Leadership
- Spirituality
- Business
- Relationships
- Parenting
- Education

- Personal growth
- Entrepreneurship
- Finance
- Sports
- Retirement planning
- Career development
- Pet care
- Sales/Marketing
- Health/Wellness
- Grief recovery
- Humor
- …and many more!

Now that we're clear on who this tool is for, before we move on I'd like to ask you to give this your complete focus. You might even want to put your phone in "do not disturb" mode. If you're reading in a noisy area, please put on your headphones or close the door. Treat these pages with the same respect you would treat me if we were discussing this in person. This is about you and your book. It's not something to take lightly.

I've authored and co-authored more than a dozen books, many of which have won prestigious awards and become best-sellers. And with those books I've launched six- and seven-figure businesses. My books have appeared in the *L. A. Times, Entrepreneur Magazine, Forbes. com* and *Huffington Post*. I've spoken on local and national TV and on stages across the U.S. My author trainings have reached nearly 80,000 people in 127 countries as of this writing. And if there's anything I've learned through it all, it's this: A book is the best way to turn your expertise into rocket fuel for your business and send your message out into the world.

I've personally done this twice. The first time I grossed half-a-million dollars. The second time I grew my business to just over a million in annual revenue, which was the result of impacting thousands of lives. It all began with the blueprint I'm about to share with you.

If you haven't downloaded the Transformation Quadrant Workbook yet, please do that now. It's free and available at *www.christinekloser.com/tq.*

CHAPTER 2

The Transformation Quadrant

You now know that without the Transformation Quadrant it's pretty much impossible to write a great book in the transformational space, which is what I call the genres for authors who want to affect true change in the world. We're called Transformational Authors, which is distinctly different from trade-fiction authors and regular nonfiction authors.

You now know this blueprint helps set the foundation, the soul, the DNA for your book. It has the power to help you overcome self-doubt, excuses and overwhelm. From this one blueprint you can gain the inspiration to create your outline, structure, marketing strategies, and everything else for your message and your book-based business.

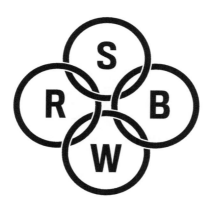

You can see why it's called the Transformation Quadrant! If you haven't yet downloaded your Transformation Quadrant Workbook at *www.christinekloser.com/tq*, I highly recommend you do that now. It'll provide an easy way to work through the Quadrant as you read along.

As you can see, there are four letters that represent the quadrants. The quadrants work together holistically, and if you're missing any one of them, you're setting yourself up for failure when you sit down to write your book. I've seen it happen over and over again. Not connecting the dots between the quadrants can stop you in your tracks; or worse yet can lead you to writing the "wrong book."

I was at an event in San Diego talking with a yoga teacher who was thrilled to have written and published her book. But as we talked more, she started tearing up. I asked her what the tears were about, and she told me she was beginning to realize how much time, energy and money she wasted writing the wrong book – a book that would never help her achieve her business goals. Even though she had hired a book coach, they never dug deep enough to build the core foundation first. By the end of our conversation I was in tears too. I knew her pain personally.

In my earlier career – before I created the original version of the tool I'm about to teach you, I had the same thing happen to me, and it's debilitating. I've "failed" so terribly in the past that I ended up having to shut down my business. I lost my home and went through bankruptcy. And I've even had business partners pull the rug out from under me. I've been through a lot in my twenty-seven years as an entrepreneur, and I know things would have been a *lot* different if I had had the Transformation Quadrant back then. It wasn't until I developed and fully understood this tool that I built my business to over one million dollars.

Take a look at my very first book called *Inspiration to Realization.*

It's an anthology that came out in 2004. It had taken me twelve years to finally strike up the courage to get my message published, and the only way I was able to do it was to write my chapter alongside thirty-nine other women who trusted me to publish their messages, too.

Thankfully it was a success, and it was written up in the print edition of *Entrepreneur Magazine* as one of the best summer reads for women in business. Because of that a lot of the members of my Network for Empowering Women Entrepreneurs asked me to help them write their books.

But I said no! I didn't know how to write a full book. My first book was beginner's luck, and

I only had to write *one* chapter! But they kept asking me – for three years… and I kept saying no.

That all changed in Marina Del Rey, California, in 2007. I was at a seminar in a room with floor-to-ceiling windows overlooking the marina. The sky was bright blue and the water was sparkling in the sunshine. You could even hear the little ding, ding, ding of the sailboats at the dock. It was awesome, and I remember it like it was yesterday. On that day, which I believe was a divinely ordained day, two of my anthology clients – separately but simultaneously – literally begged me to help them write their books.

Have you ever had one of those moments when your mouth was moving faster than your brain? Well, I don't know why, but I said yes to them: that I'd help them write their books! It was crazy because I was running an anthology publishing company and a large community for conscious entrepreneurs. I was busy as heck. Not to mention that my daughter Janet was only two years old at the time, so I had a toddler underfoot 24/7!

But that's not even the craziest part. After saying yes to those two clients I said yes to four other people too! What's more is I threw out a five-figure price tag for my new book-writing program, and they all said yes!

I now had to figure out how to teach someone to write a book, and the best way I knew was to write my own book. I'm not one of those people who can teach something if I haven't done it myself first.

I love to go to the spa to think things through. I do my best creative work there. So I went to my favorite spa to figure out how to write a book. As I sat by the indoor pool, I closed my eyes, took a few deep breaths and asked the universe to "Show me where to start. Show me what to do."

I had my spiral notebook open, my favorite purple pen in my hand, and I just kept asking for guidance, quite honestly with a little bit of desperation, because I had my first class coming up in a matter of days and I needed to know what to teach!

Thankfully the clarity started to come. I could feel the excitement building and I just kept writing down everything that came. I kept asking, "What's the next step?" "What's the next step?" This process continued until the sun set and the pool was about to close, and by the time they kicked me out I had the name of the program and the curriculum for the program, and I had even registered the domain for the program.

Now it was time to put it to the test. I was going to be my own guinea pig. And boy, oh boy... did it work. Take a look. This is my second book which came out in 2008.

It got endorsed by top thought leaders like Neale Donald Walsch, Arielle Ford, Michael Gerber, Mark Victor Hansen and many others. It won awards and became a best-seller on Amazon – overall, not just in some obscure category. It was in the top 100 print books on all of Amazon!

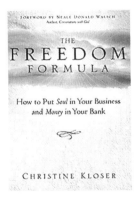

I leveraged that book to sell out my first three-day seminar in 2009 and generate a half a million dollars in new revenue. That was the most money I'd ever made in a year, let alone three days. And it all happened within six months of *The Freedom Formula* being published.

If you're not sold yet on how a book can start, grow and take you and your business to the next level, I don't know what will sell you on it. But unfortunately I didn't have my Transformation Quadrant in place back then. Little did I know that this was the beginning of the end. I thought to myself, "I made it." I was successful! But then I started to have those kinds of days when I just couldn't get out of bed. I stayed in my bathrobe feeling depressed and trying to figure out what happened and why it didn't feel amazing. How could I experience that level of success and yet be so unhappy and unfulfilled?

In retrospect, the answer was simple. I didn't have the Transformation Quadrant, and as a result I had written the wrong book and had created the wrong business, which attracted some extremely challenging clients into my life. Some were lazy, they were demanding, and they didn't take action on my coaching. Some didn't do what we agreed they would do, and when they didn't get their desired results they'd blamed me! I woke up with a feeling of dread almost every day.

That's why I really dislike programs that say "Write a book in seventy-two hours. Become a best-seller overnight." None of them ask you, the author, if you're writing the right book, on the right foundation, that will sustain you and bring you joy in your work for years to come. The Transformation Quadrant prevents you from falling into that trap. And what a trap.

Back to my story. In mid-2009, about six months after my half-million-dollar event, I started terminating those challenging clients and refunding their money – lots of it. I knew the impact would be substantial for me and my family, but I just couldn't continue with the wrong foundation, the wrong message and the wrong clients at that time in my career. I had to reset.

I shut down my business and took time off. I knew I had to dive deeper and reevaluate my work, my message, my priorities and my business if I ever wanted to succeed for real. And that's what I did. As I was going through the bankruptcy and foreclosure I mentioned earlier, I dropped to my knees and went back to my roots. I knew teaching people how to write books and grow their businesses was great, but something essential was missing for me and those I wanted to serve. I came up with the first version of the Transformation Quadrant in 2011 after two rigorous years of soul-searching:

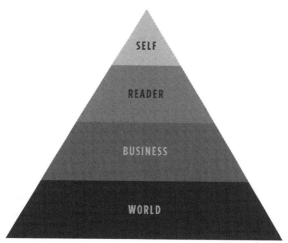

Again, I used myself as a guinea pig. And within three months of discovering and defining this first version of the Quadrant for myself and the people I wanted to help, I had trained nearly 10,000 authors around the world on this very topic. It earned a relatively quick six figures, which in a few years evolved into a million-dollar coaching, consulting and publishing business serving Transformational Authors around the globe. This time I was financially successful and fulfilled and happy. And it was because I built that business on my Transformation Quadrant blueprint.

So what exactly is the Transformation Quadrant and what do the four letters stand for? As you know, DNA is the blueprint for every single part in your body. It tells your body how to "write" new cells for every "passage" and "chapter" in your body. It's the foundation embedded in every function and component.

That's what the Transformation Quadrant is for your book. It's not four separate parts, sections or chapters. It's four threads, if you will, that are woven together throughout your book and the business you build around it. If you're missing any one or more of these threads, your book, message and business can fall apart. This is what happened to my first book-based business, so it's critical to take the time to think about each thread – each quadrant – and how they work together to weave the tapestry of your goals and dreams.

Each thread is represented by a letter with its own square in the Transformation Quadrant. They are S, R, B and W.

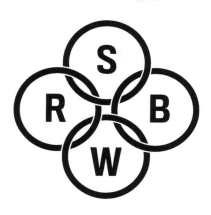

Most Transformational Authors start in the "R" quadrant, which stands for Reader. Obviously you want people to read your book. You want to change, impact and transform your readers' lives. That's the definition of a Transformational Author – you want to impact and transform lives. But you can't focus solely on your reader. The other three quadrants are equally important!

"S" stands for Self, "B" stands for Business and "W" stands for World. You must address all four quadrants together as one whole. The B quadrant is also pretty straightforward. If you really want to impact lives in a profound way in today's world, it's not enough to write a book. You need to get your message out there and do deeper work through your business by creating seminars, consulting, workshops, courses, marketing content and speaking topics *based on your book*.

After all, the vast majority of authors don't make a living selling books. And if you can't make a living doing your work, then you can't keep spreading your message and impacting more lives. You want to think about the transformation you'd like to see in your business as a result of writing your book. So that's B for Business.

Nearly every author I've met wants to positively impact the world with their message, so "W" in the quadrant stands for World. We don't just want our readers' lives to transform; we want to have a ripple effect of positive change through each reader and into the lives they impact. It's not enough to focus only on transforming your readers' lives but also to have a larger impact in the world as a result of your book being in it.

These three quadrants – Reader, Business and World – are vital, but what can trip you up the most is if you miss the "S" quadrant. "S" stands for Self. As you might have noticed, the Transformation Quadrant is about transformation. And each quadrant is about transforming something – your readers, your business, the world. But those are all external things, and if you focus only on message, money and impact you leave out the key ingredient that makes it all possible: The human underneath it all. The literal soul in your book. You! Before you change your readers' lives, impact the world and build or expand your business, ask yourself, "What's the transformation I want to experience in me?"

We've all heard the stories: people achieving their life goals; people at the top of their game; people who are the "best" in the world – yet they're unhappy. They have a successful career; they have a fulfilling family life; they do work that impacts lives – but they forgot about themselves and what they *truly* want. I don't want that for you.

Writing a book, building a business, creating a product or course – it's challenging, difficult work. It'll test you. You can push through and ignore the Self quadrant to focus on your message, but you'll most likely end up miserable like the woman I met at the seminar in San Diego, or like I was after writing *The Freedom Formula*.

But if you use the Transformation Quadrant to think through all four threads and how they connect to each other *before* you sit down to write, plan, and strategize, you'll build something that's holistic – something that will bring success, fulfillment and happiness. And it will be *sustainable*. You won't burn out, go broke or break down.

It's interesting that when all four quadrants are working together, the universe answers in amazing ways. It doesn't matter what your religion or belief system is – you can call it synchronicity, God, karma, or a miracle – but what happens is that people show up. Connections are made. New opportunities become available.

One of my clients, Gail Saunders, after her husband died, wrote a book about dealing with the loss of a loved one. Because she focused on all four quadrants, she wrote a powerful book called *Resilient Heart*. It's so good that a university called her asking for permission to make it mandatory reading for a psychology class.

Think about that... Gail never imagined something like that was even possible. But that's what happens when you build on the blueprint that the Transformation Quadrant provides.

Another client, Eileen Santos, who wrote *Unmasking Your Soul,* received calls from community leaders and event producers. They wanted her to speak about her book and even to host private workshops for them. As you can see, the Transformation Quadrant really works! But you must look at all the pieces and how they relate to each other, which is what we'll cover in the next chapter.

CHAPTER 3

How the Quadrants Work Together

When you divide the Transformation Quadrant into halves horizontally, you can see a deeper dynamic to take this powerful tool and your book even further. If you write a book or create a product only for personal and material reasons like making money and boosting your image, you're focusing on only the top half of the blueprint (Self and Business). A lot of today's "microwave-method" author programs focus on this: "Just get a book out there; it doesn't matter if it's good or not." You might game the system and become an Amazon best-seller. Maybe some people will be impressed you wrote a book. But it's a shell game. When someone opens your book they'll see it's not very good... because you missed the Reader and World quadrants. You didn't really connect with the reader or provide the highest value for them. You missed an amazing experience and a driver for your business: your raving fans. Nobody's going to rave about your book if you don't focus on delivering value and connecting with the transformation you want for your reader and the world in the first place!

But the flip side is just as dangerous! Let's say you're focused only on the other half. Leaving your own transformation out of the book will cause you to miss out on the boost of confidence, clarity and courage that only writing a book can bring, and your readers will miss out on truly connecting with you and feeling your heart and soul in the book. You'll also miss out on transforming your business by means of your book.

As you can see, both halves should work together. That's the power of the Transformation Quadrant. You can't ignore even one of them.

You can break the Transformation Quadrant in half the other way, too. (Again, if you don't have the workbook yet, download it now at *www.christinekloser.com/tq*. It'll make it much easier to follow along as you read.) Let's say you focus on you and your readers in the top and left quadrants. You'll grow personally, and you'll have a message that changes your readers' lives, but what you'll be missing on the right side are the practical and tangible aspects of writing your book. These are the two quadrants that help you get more readers, impact more lives and turn your book into a business (or enhance your existing business) so you can support yourself doing work you love!

Let's look at what happens when you're too focused on the: Business and World quandrants. Let's say you're a rock star when it comes to business and marketing your message. You know how to build lists, find joint-venture partners, generate traffic, create programs, get speaking gigs, etc. You have a valuable message and it has the potential to start a movement.

But if you don't connect with your readers and you're not deeply connected with your self, your venture in writing a book is going to sputter and fail. You might gain some traction, but it'll soon collapse because the heart and soul – the DNA – is missing. Or worse, if it goes viral and you get a tremendous amount of attention, you might not be ready to handle the growth, and collapse under it because you didn't transform yourself as you wrote your book. All four quadrants must be in place and working together like well-oiled parts of a unified machine.

~◡

So let's get started on your Transformation Quadrant! Pull out your workbook. (If you haven't downloaded the workbook from *www.christinekloser.com/tq*, get out a piece of paper and draw a simple four circle quadrant like the previously shown TQ model.)

Write "Self," "Reader," "Business" and "World" next to each quadrant.

Write a few notes for each quadrant about the kind of transformation you want in that quadrant. In other words, answer each of these questions:

1) What transformation do you want for your SELF through the process of writing your book?

2) What transformation do you want your READER to experience?

3) What transformation do you want for your BUSINESS as a result of writing your book?

4) What transformation do you want your book to inspire in the WORLD?

As you answer these questions and nail down the Transformation Quadrant for your book, you're going to gain clarity about your message, your content, and the business you can build around your book. If you already have a business, you'll begin to see how to expand it as an author.

You'll likely start to see what the marketing will look like. If you don't have a title for your book yet, it might show up as you ponder these questions. That's the power of having this blueprint in place. It's holistic. It creates a solid foundation for maximum success. A lot of author programs miss out on one, two or even three of the quadrants.

Pushy, money-hungry coaches are all about business. They want you to write a cookie-cutter book based on their favorite formula. But that approach simply can't deliver your best work. It's just missing too much.

On the flip side, there are "spiritual" book coaches who have you do all the inner work but don't know the first thing about the Business quadrant and truly making an impact in the world.

And there are those "writerly" coaches. They're so deep into grammar and sentence structure that they forget the transformation that's required from the author first.

I think you get the picture. The bottom line is you shouldn't write a single word of your manuscript until you're crystal clear on the Transformation Quadrant for your book. When you do this right the Quadrant becomes your book's "north star." (If you're sold on the Quadrant but not sure how to get started, later in the book I share how you can consult with me privately to nail down the Transformation Quadrant for your book.)

So far I've been explaining this tool in an abstract way, so now let's look at it on a practical level. I'm going to use my client Colleen O'Grady as an example. She wrote a book called *Dial Down the Drama*. It's a parenting book for mothers of teenaged daughters.

I'll start with her readers. She wanted to empower frustrated, burned-out mothers of teenaged daughters to maintain good relationships and solid mother-daughter connections through the teen years. I have a teenaged daughter myself; I read Colleen's book, and it's amazing.

But what about the Self quadrant? Have you heard the adage "You teach what you most need to learn"? This realization comes to a lot of authors, just as it did for Colleen. For her "S" quadrant she wanted to release "imposter syndrome" and embrace her authentic self by acknowledging that she didn't have to be the perfect mother in order to write a great book for moms!

The transformation she wanted in her Business quadrant was to become a well-known authority and respected expert in her field. She also wanted to attract more media attention and speaking engagements to grow her private practice.

And as for Colleen's World quadrant, her vision was to bring more peace and harmony to all mother – teenaged daughter relationships, and in doing so bring more peace to the world.

I'll share the results she got in the next chapter, but hopefully you can see from this example how each of the four quadrants are woven together to create one solid foundation: the DNA that leads to results on every level.

CHAPTER 4

Solving "The Big Three" Author Challenges

The beautiful thing about the Transformation Quadrant is that it does a lot more than create the blueprint for your book. Remember the top three challenges (or blocks) authors face that I mentioned above – overwhelm, self-doubt and lack of time? You'll be happy to know that you can use the Quadrant to solve these challenges, too.

I'll start with overwhelm and confusion – the voice that says, "How do I start? What do I do? I'm confused!" This voice chimes in when you're not clear about the core message of your book. But if you've used the Quadrant to get your book's DNA down, questions like this disappear.

Be warned, however, that as you dig deep to create your Transformation Quadrant you might find yourself touching on some challenging topics. I get that. And the Quadrant is *designed* to get you to dig deep enough to reach the core of your message and your self! Some authors, even those who have been sitting on their messages for years, can rattle off profound answers and gain tremendous clarity in each quadrant in fifteen minutes. You might be one of them – or not, and that's okay. It might take you an hour or a week. But this kind of inquiry you must do. It's exactly the work I do with my clients. I ask the direct, tough questions.

Nothing gets me more riled up than book coaches who only scratch the surface, then push you through their "perfect" system and you end up with a microwaved, formulaic book. You can see now that the Transformation Quadrant is decidedly not a formula. It's a tool for accessing the depth and totality of *your* book. I push my clients to dive deeper. The last thing I want is for you to write the wrong book like that yoga teacher did, and like I did earlier in my career. I nudge and ask direct, clarifying questions, and that's why I get emails from clients saying, "Thanks for pushing me to get more clarity on my book. I would've written the wrong book if you hadn't held my feet to the fire." Clarity is an amazing thing.

For example, my client, Dallas Travers, had a lot of difficulty starting her book, but she knew it would change her business forever. We worked on her four quadrants, and her book, *The Tao of Show Business*, sold 50,000 copies, and Dallas became a leader in her field and grew her business to nearly seven figures! But here's what I love most: She recognized the importance of the work we did in the Self quadrant and wrote me a thank-you letter saying, "Your powerful process completely transformed who I see myself to be in the world." That's the best kind of letter I could have received!

Then there's Gerry. When Gerry first found me he was on the verge of throwing away his manuscript. He hated it. He told me, "Nobody's going to read this. It's no good." He had a lot of self-doubt. The problem was he didn't have the kind of blueprint he needed. The message itself was valuable, but Gerry was all over the place with it. I showed him the Transformation Quadrant, which is when everything clicked for him. And guess what. His book *Messages from Margaret* got published by Hay House – his dream publisher! Not only that, they published his second book, too, and he now has his own show on Hay House Radio impacting lives around the world.

As you can see, the Quadrant can help you with the challenge of overwhelm and confusion. But what about having enough time? You're probably asking, "How can the Transformation Quadrant help me with that?" Well, it's not a time machine, but it's something close. We all have the same twenty-four hours in a day, but some people accomplish more with them. The question is how.

It comes down to the "internal shifts" that the Self quadrant can activate. People are always talking about time management, but it's really about *energy management*. How many times have you planned to write but found some excuse not to? Maybe you dread staring at a blank page. Maybe you'd rather organize your sock drawer than write! I propose that you *do* have time, and that it's not time you're lacking, but energy. And guess what the best energy source is when you're writing a book. If you guessed the Transformation Quadrant, you're absolutely right.

When you've done your Transformation Quadrant correctly you enjoy a renewed sense of clarity, focus, confidence, direction, motivation and vision for your book. This is what fuels your energy, which allows you to *make* time to write. Suddenly you're okay with putting in an hour after the kids are in bed, or waking up at 5:00 in the morning to get some writing in. Believe it or not, you might even look forward to squeezing in these times to write. The Transformation Quadrant is that powerful... once it's clear.

I have a client, Dan, who was struggling big time. He'd sit down to write and nothing would come out. He felt like he was up against a wall. We worked on his Transformation Quadrant and he went from writing 100 words in a month to writing thousands of words that month. Last I heard he'd written nearly 20,000 words of his book. This happened because he was willing to reorganize his thinking process. I pushed him lovingly, yet directly, and things changed for him. The Transformation Quadrant – when you do it right – transforms you.

Beth Ellen is another client. She was already working sixty hours a week running her online school, Wings to Soar Academy. When we first started talking she doubted she had time to write a book. She had a business, students, staff, curriculum to develop... and she was speaking at education conferences in many different locations. But she said yes to her book, we worked on the Quadrant together, and she found time to write. The book was aligned with her business, her self, her customers and the change she wanted to bring to the world. It's now an Amazon best-seller, and it consistently attracts new students to her school. That's the beauty of a book!

We've covered overwhelm and lack of time, but the worst of the three big challenges authors face is self-doubt. And I want to draw a distinction here: I think a lot of self-doubt is actually masking the "what if" syndrome. It sounds like this: "What if I write this book and it flops?" "What if I waste all this time?" "What if it's not good enough?" I think nearly every author on this planet experiences this.

Even *New York Times* best-selling authors have confided in me that they have fears about writing. They deal with "what if" syndrome too. They say to themselves, "What if they find out I'm an imposter?" "What if my book is crap compared to the thousand others on the same topic?" "What if my family rejects me?" The list goes on... I've heard it all, helped others get past it, and even dealt with it myself.

My parents are wonderful, and did the best they could, but I grew up in a "seen but not heard" household in which my father was the authority. His voice boomed like a bass drum, and I felt that my voice, thoughts and feelings didn't matter. As the middle child I learned to swallow my words and do my best to keep the peace. I never even dared to ask "what if." The idea of speaking up and using my voice didn't even occur to me; I just wanted to stay in the shadows and not have my dad's yelling directed at me.

I didn't get over this fear until I moved 3,000 miles away and worked on my Self quadrant. And I wouldn't have written a dozen books if I had never worked to liberate my voice and gain the confidence to share it!

The Transformation Quadrant is a great tool to help you get past "what if" syndrome and any other self-doubt you may face.

My client, Katye Anna, for example, wanted to write books for decades, but never did. She wasn't sure if she was ready to be an author because she was afraid to say good-bye to her somewhat isolated, safe and comfortable life. For the most part she was content with the small, private practice she maintained in her home. But deep inside she could feel herself being called to something bigger.

We worked together and she got past her self-doubts and "what if" syndrome. She has now authored six books, and has many more in the works. And her small, local practice has expanded across the United States and around the globe. What's more, she hosts retreats, teaches several online programs and has even gone on tour for weeks at a time to speak and present workshops about her books. She experienced a 180-degree shift.

And then there's Lilia. She had a very different "what if" going on. She wrote a book called *The Art of Listening to Angels*. She was an attorney working for the U.S. government, but she secretly talked to angels. You're probably thinking that those two worlds just don't mesh, and Lilia was afraid of "coming out" with the truth about her angels.

What she really wanted was to leave law behind and build a mission-driven, book-based business. We worked together, using the Transformation Quadrant, and she was able to write and publish her book, quit her job, create and teach an online "angel" course, host workshops and build a business doing what she loves with clients she loves.

Finally, let's continue with Colleen, who wrote *Dial Down the Drama* for mothers of teenaged daughters. After we worked together on her Quadrant and she had written her book, she got a nice publishing deal with a traditional publisher. She also received lots of media exposure and even did a TEDx talk. She's impacting mothers around the world now. The last time I spoke with her she was celebrating her book being published in Chinese!

Colleen is having massive impact, but a couple of years ago you'd never have believed it. At one of my retreats she sat cross-legged with her notebook open, her pen dangling in her hand and her head bowed – in tears. This woman, who now does amazing work in the world, was in the throes of the pain of imposter syndrome because right before she came to the retreat she had an argument with her daughter. And all she could think to herself was "What if they find out I'm not a perfect mom?" "Who's going to listen to what I have to say?" "What if they find out that I raise my voice at times?" What if, what if, what if.

And those "what ifs," honest to goodness, could have kept her down forever. But thankfully we got to work together and get her past that doubt, and now you know her results.

If you have any self-doubts, think you're an imposter, or don't think your book is worth writing, I can guarantee you that once you nail down your Transformation Quadrant, those things will belong to the past.

CHAPTER 5

Putting the Quadrant to Work for You

I imagine that by now you're grasping the power of the Transformation Quadrant. And I hope you've started working on yours already using the free workbook at *www.christinekloser.com/tq*. My goal is to show you how this blueprint can be the DNA of your message, your book and your business. You now understand how the Quadrant builds on itself and empowers you to overcome your fears and finally write your *best* book! It does all this, and even more…

You can also use it to write your book's back cover – the most important 250 words you'll write for your book.

It can help you discover your unique, "trademarkable" technology. Trademarking their technology is something a lot of my clients never realized they could do! Many of them followed my coaching and in fact have registered trademarks for their method, system or process.

You can also use your Quadrant to uncover ways to create secondary income from your book, such as courses, speaking and consulting.

And, of course, you can create a clear and effective book outline based on your Quadrant. Whenever my clients get stuck, we revisit their Transformation Quadrant and the creative inspiration is there.

The clincher is that you must create your Transformation Quadrant *correctly* or you'll build everything on a faulty foundation – on DNA that "writes" the wrong thing into all you do to write, publish and promote your book.

Creating the Transformation Quadrant is some of the most powerful work I do with my clients at the beginning of our journeys together. Get it right and everything else falls into place! Get it wrong and you can end up where I did after *The Freedom Formula* came out. That's why I'm on a mission to make sure no one goes through the pain I did, and to ensure that authors around the world create Quadrants that are right for them!

Remember when I referred to "You teach what you most need to learn"? I recently went on a four-day strategy retreat with my marketing consultant. We worked on my Transformation Quadrant, and I gained two important insights. One, I had not been taking full ownership of my Business quadrant. For the past couple of years I have drifted a little from my core mission and purpose and made some misaligned decisions in my business. And this happened because I lost sight of my Business quadrant.

This can happen to you, too. Creating your Quadrant is not a one-time event. It's important to revisit it over and over again as you grow, shift and evolve.

The second insight from revisiting my Transformation Quadrant is that I do my best work in private coaching calls, live events, and when working in person with a client. When I give a client my focus, attention and energy in those ways, I can see and sense what's going on with them, hear between their words and ask the delicate and difficult questions that create clarity, inspiration and direction. As a result of this deeper work, they experience amazing breakthroughs in every quadrant! And I love every minute of it!

I've always known that my gift is working with people in a deep, personal way. Heck, I've been facilitating transformation events since 1997. I got this! But you can know something and yet not *really* know it, which means you're not taking full advantage of it. I kept building out my online programs and webinars to sell more courses, but it was somewhat haphazard and all over the place. And worst of all, it was draining for me. Then I would get on the phone with a coaching client, or facilitate an author retreat, and I was suddenly rejuvenated, energized and felt like I was doing what I was put on this planet to do.

During that retreat my marketing guy straight-out asked me, "Christine, all your best clients; the ones who have written their books and are growing book-based businesses; the ones you *loved* working with; the ones you connected most deeply with… who are they?" He made me list them, totally putting me on the spot.

First I told him about Sue Salvemini, author of *Leadership by Choice.* She's a leadership consultant who finished writing her first draft in thirty-three days to get it done for a speaking engagement in front of 400 of her ideal clients. She was awesome to work with!

Then there was Christine Rosas, author of *The Sensitive Edge.* At one point she really didn't think she could write her book, but we worked through it together and now she's launched her speaking career and is fulfilling her mission. We're friends for life!

Next I told him about Beth Kennedy, author of *Career Recharge.* She's a corporate coach who booked her first international speaking gig before her book was even finished! Just the fact that she was a forthcoming author who knew exactly what her book was about in all four quadrants got her the gig. She was a highly focused woman on a mission. And a ton of fun to coach!

I also talked about Don Awalt, author of *The Uncomfortable Zone,* who is a corporate executive on a mission to help people get comfortable with being uncomfortable. Don leveraged his book to schedule several speaking engagements and open doors to audiences of 800-1000 of his ideal customers. Pretty impressive! Wouldn't you agree?

I told him about the author of *Lost and Found,* Ellen Monsees, who finished the first draft of her manuscript at one of my retreats. We had a blast celebrating together. She's not the same woman she was when we started working together! Nor is her business the same. She's quadrupled the number of clients she sees at her new office. She's writing her second book now.

I could go on, but you get the picture. What all five of those authors – and many others – have in common is that they didn't struggle alone to figure out their Quadrant or how to write their books. They worked with me and my team to be supported every step of the way. They were either coached by me privately or in group coaching calls, came to my in-person retreats, attended virtual retreats or checked in with us on a weekly basis so they were held accountable to what they said they were going to do for their book.

It's this kind of connection and support that ensures you don't just jot down some notes in your Transformation Quadrant and that's the end of it. When you stay connected and supported in a way that's the best fit for you and your book, you become unstoppable! No doubt or fear can keep you from writing. No time crunch can sidetrack you. No confusion can keep you stuck. No matter what you're going through with your book, you just can't fail when you have a coach in your corner showing you what to do every step of the way.

Some of the clients on my list joined my Mastermind. They not only wanted to be coached by me, but also wanted to be part of a community of like-minded people who were also taking action on their book-writing goals. Others worked with me privately. They knew they wanted me to walk them step by step through every twist and turn of the book-writing process – even being able to send me emergency emails or text messages if they really needed help. They knew they did better one on one than in groups, and understood how much faster and further they could go with private mentorship.

Why am I telling you this? Because I don't have a "one size fits all" coaching and consulting process like many coaches out there. I know that every author is different and must find the structure, coaching and support that are right for them and their book. Otherwise it's like trying to fit a square peg into a round hole; it doesn't work – not to mention that it hurts and can be quite costly!

For some people the right fit is my award-winning Get Your Book Done® program. In fact I recently received this email from a graduate, Jean-Ann:

"I'm thrilled to say my book, *Living Life From The Inside Out,* was published! The early sales have been better than expected and the feedback has been fantastic! I highly recommend this program to anyone interested in writing and publishing their book. I'm so glad I found Get Your Book Done and even happier to say I Got It Done!"

My team and I are here to help. What I've covered about the powerful Transformation Quadrant is just the tip of the iceberg, and I want it to be the beginning of our journey in supporting your author success!

Too many people read books like *The Transformation Quadrant* with hope and enthusiasm, as you may be doing right now, but never take action. I want more for you than that! If you're reading this because you have a dream to really do something with your book – to make a difference and impact lives with your message while enjoying the benefits that only authorship can bring, like authority, visibility, credibility, confidence, clarity, courage and clients – I don't want you to feel lost, alone, confused or frustrated. And I certainly don't want someone else to guide you down the wrong path, like the woman I met in San Diego and so many others. Because it doesn't have to be like that.

You don't have to be one of the sad folks who wanted to write a book but ended up taking it to the grave with them. I realize that's a strong statement, but if not now, then when? What will it take for you to step firmly onto your path to becoming a Transformational Author? Hasn't it been long enough already?

I'm here to help you every step of the way, with the Transformation Quadrant being the first step you take. And if you want to learn how I can help you take the *next* step, keep reading!

CONSULT WITH CHRISTINE

Hopefully this proposal will help you take the next step in putting the power of the Transformation Quadrant to work for you: You and I should hop on a private call, and together, with my undivided attention for a full forty-five minutes, we can nail down *your* Transformation Quadrant.

Having my expert guidance to ensure you do this right will be a game-changer for you and your book. And it will give us a chance to discuss any further support you might need to achieve your author goals – but we won't be able to do that unless we talk.

As you can imagine, my schedule is quite full, and there are only a small number of spots available for private consultations each month. They are both time- and energy-intensive! A private, one-time consultation with me at this level is normally $997. But for readers of *The Transformation Quadrant* I'm offering a special $500 discount, so the consultation will be only $497.

I'm going to do one more thing to make this as risk-free as possible for you. The consultation you'll book at *www.christinekloser.com/consult* comes with a twenty-minute "safe switch." If by the twenty-minute mark you don't feel like you've received value, you can stop the call immediately and ask for a refund. The risk is all on me, because I'm committed to helping you!

As I said, this is a very time- and energy-intensive consultation, and I don't have a lot of openings in my calendar, so if you want a consultation you'll want to go to this page now.

www.christinekloser.com/consult

When you land there, click the pink button

that says "Click Here for Your Private Consultation with Christine." Then fill in your contact and payment information. Next there's a short preparatory form to ensure we're both prepared for you to get tons of value during our call. After you send me this form you'll go to my calendar where you'll choose a date and time for our call.

After your private consultation there are two possible outcomes: One, you will have gained all the clarity you need, and as a self-starter you'll write your book on your own. Or you might realize how valuable it is to have coaching, guidance and ongoing support for writing your book, in which case I'll apply the full fee for the consultation to any of my other programs.

As I said, I don't have a one-size-fits-all process because no two authors are exactly alike. My team and I are here to help as many people as we can write their transformational books and make a difference in the world, and we'll ensure that you find the best fit to make that dream a reality.

If you're on the fence, let me ask you this: Did you learn something reading this book that'll help you write your book? Did you resonate with the Transformation Quadrant? And do you now see the amazing potential for you, your book and your business? If so, imagine what'll happen when we work together during your private consultation… and possibly beyond!

That's where it all begins. And it would be my pleasure to serve you more deeply.

www.christinekloser.com/consult

Thank you for reading *The Transformation Quadrant*. I look forward to talking with you soon!

Will You Post A Review on Amazon?
If you like what you read in
The Transformation Quadrant, I'd greatly appreciate
if you'd post a review on Amazon. This will
help me reach more people
with this message. Thank you!
Go here to post your review:
www.tq-review.com

AUTHOR RESOURCES

Work hands-on with me
Private coaching and consulting to create the transformational book, business and life you were born for.
Email: *support@christinekloser.com*

Discover *Publishing Power*
This free guide will help you avoid the top five mistakes authors make when it comes to publishing their book.
www.christinekloser.com/publishing-power

Enroll in my award-winning *Get Your Book Done*® program
Everything you need to write your transformational book using my easy-to-follow yet organic and natural writing process.
www.getyourbookdone.com

Grab a copy of my award-winning book,
An invaluable resource for conscious business owners. Plus, it's a great model to review as you develop your own book.
www.thefreedomformula.com

Mailing Address:
Christine Kloser Companies LLC
211 Pauline Drive #513
York, PA 16402

Phone:
(800) 930-3713

Email:
support@christinekloser.com

Website:
www.christinekloser.com

Social Media:
Facebook: *www.facebook.com/christinekloser*
Twitter: *www.twitter.com/christinekloser*
LinkedIn: *www.linkedin.com/in/christinekloser*

73698987R00038

Made in the
USA
Middletown, DE